Prehistoric Creatures Then and Now

ICHTHYOSAURUS

By K.S. Rodriguez

Illustrated by Greg Harris

Steadwell
Books

Raintree Steck-Vaughn Publishers

A Harcourt Company

Austin · New York
www.steck-vaughn.com

J

For William Arthur Squires, with love
Special thanks to Paul Marsh, Paleontology Researcher,
American Museum of Natural History

Produced by By George Productions, Inc.

Published by Raintree Steck-Vaughn Publishers,
an imprint of Steck-Vaughn Company

Library of Congress Cataloging-in-Publication Data
Rodriguez, K.S.
    Ichthyosaurus / K.S. Rodriguez
        p.   cm — (Prehistoric creatures then and now)
    Summary: Introduces the "fish lizard" that lived in the world's
oceans during the age of dinosaurs. Includes index.
    ISBN 0-7398-0099-X
    Ichthyosaurus — Juvenile literature. [1. Ichthyosaurus.
2. Prehistoric animals.]   I. Title. II. Series.
    QE862.I2 R63   2000
    567.9'37 — dc21   99-055474

Printed and bound in the United States of America
10 9 8 7 6 5 4 3 2 1 LB 03 02 01 00

Photo Acknowledgments:
Pages 4–5: The Field Museum, photo by John Weinstein; pages
12–13, 16: Department of Library Services, American Museum of
Natural History; page 26: Royal Tyrrell Museum of
Paleontology/Alberta Community Development.

Contents

Ichthyosaurs Ruled the Sea

4

Hundreds of millions of years ago, long before there were human beings, dinosaurs roamed the earth. Other creatures swam the seas. These sea creatures were called ichthyosaurs. Ichthyosaurus belonged to this group.

A painting showing ichthyosaurs and other prehistoric creatures (from the Field Museum, Chicago)

Ichthyosaur means "fish lizard." These creatures lived in the earth's oceans about 245 million to 95 million years ago. They lived during the "Age of the Dinosaurs." But they were not dinosaurs.

Dinosaurs lived only on land. Even though ichthyosaurs lived in the water, they were not fish.

Time Line

Mesozoic
(The era of the dinosaurs)

prosauropod

Stegosaurus

Tyrannosaurus

Triassic
245 million to
208 million
years ago

Jurassic
208 million to
145 million
years ago

Cretaceous
145 million to
65 million
years ago

 6

Ichthyosaurs were reptiles. They did not have gills. They had lungs to breathe air.

There were many kinds of ichthyosaurs. They came in different shapes and sizes. There were so many, in fact, you could say they ruled the seas! But the best known ichthyosaur is the one that gave the group its name—Ichthyosaurus.

Cenozoic
(The era of mammals, including humans)

mammoth

human

Tertiary
65 million to
5 million
years ago

Quaternary
1.6 million
years ago
to today

What was Ichthyosaurus?

Ichthyosaurus lived in the oceans near what are now England, Germany, Greenland, and Canada. It lived during the Jurassic and Cretaceous periods, about 208 million to 95 million years ago.

Ichthyosaurus had long rows of very sharp teeth.

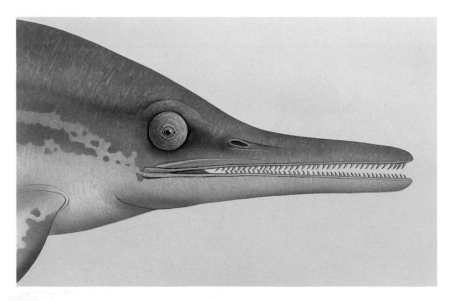

In many ways Ichthyosaurus was like ocean creatures we see today. Like a shark it had lots of long, sharp teeth. It ate other sea creatures, such as fish and squid.

And like dolphins and whales, Ichthyosaurus breathed air. It had nostrils on its head and had to swim to the surface to get air.

Like dolphins and whales, Ichthyosaurus swam to the surface to breathe air.

Ichthyosaurus swam the seas with many ▶
other prehistoric creatures.

▼ Ichthyosaurus ate other sea creatures, such as fish and squid.

Like a tuna it could swim very fast. Its strong tail and flippers helped it speed through the water.

Like a dolphin it had a dorsal fin on its back and a bottle-shaped nose. Ichthyosaurus was about as big as a dolphin, too. It was 6 to 7 feet (1.8 to 2.1 m) long.

An Ichthyosaurus fossil with skin

Scientists have learned much about Ichthyosaurus. But there are still many things they do not know.

For many years scientists wondered how Ichthyosaurus gave birth. Ichthyosaurs were reptiles, and reptiles lay eggs. Did Ichthyosaurus lay eggs in the ocean like fish? Did it crawl onto land and lay them like turtles?

Then some scientists found fossils of grown ichthyosaurs with small ichthyosaurs inside them.

An ichthyosaur fossil with its young inside

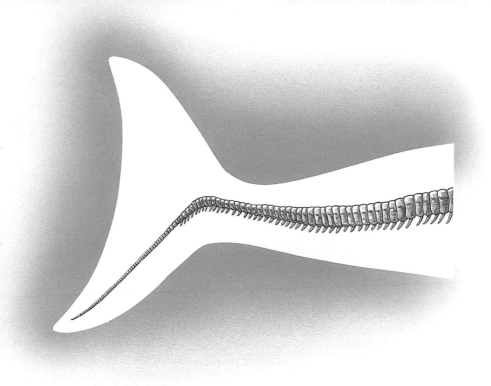

A drawing of an ichthyosaur fossil showing the tail

Fossils are records of life long ago. A fossil can be a bone or a footprint or the mark of a skeleton left in a rock. Fossils help tell a story about how a creature lived and looked.

Thanks to these fossils, scientists think they have an answer. They believe Ichthyosaurus kept its eggs inside its body until the eggs hatched. Then it gave birth to live young.

Experts believe that Ichthyosaurus kept eggs in its body until they hatched, then gave birth to live young.

At least one mystery was solved! But no one seems to have an answer to the biggest mystery of all.

The Biggest Mystery

Ichthyosaurus and other ichthyosaurs lived so long ago that it is amazing we know anything about them. Scientists called paleontologists learn what they can from fossils. Fossils tell us many things about Ichthyosaurus and other creatures. But they cannot tell us everything. So far they have not told us why ichthyosaurs disappeared.

Flippers and a strong tail helped ichthyosaurs swim very fast.

Paleontologists are starting to figure out why the dinosaurs disappeared. They think a giant rock from space, called a meteorite, hit Earth. Dust clouds blocked out sunlight. Fires destroyed the places where dinosaurs lived. Large animals such as dinosaurs were not able to live.

However, the last ichthyosaur died 30 million years before the last dinosaurs died. What happened then to kill ichthyosaurus and all the ocean reptiles? No one knows for sure.

Some paleontologists think that other meat-eating sea creatures, such as sharks, killed all ichthyosaurs or ate all their food. Volcanoes changed the oceans so much that ichthyosaurs could not live in them anymore. The change in the oceans occurred when the continents moved and mountains were pushed up. This movement created volcanoes.

Paleontologists continue to search for answers with each new fossil they find. Perhaps one day they will solve this mystery.

Sharks may have killed off the ichthyosaurs.

Mary Anning, Young Fossil Hunter

Imagine finding fossils in your own neighborhood! That is just how Ichthyosaurus was discovered.

In the early 1800s Mary Anning grew up in England, near the sea. In her town there were many fossils of ocean creatures. Her father was a cabinet maker, but his hobby was fossil hunting. Whenever she could, Mary went with him. Sometimes she took her dog and hunted for fossils by herself. If she found a fossil that was too big to carry, Mary's dog would mark the spot. Then her dog would lead Mary and her father back to the same spot later.

In 1810, when she was just 11 years old, Mary found the bones of an odd, fishlike animal. No one had ever seen fossils like these before. In time the strange "fish lizard" would be called Ichthyosaurus. Mary had discovered a whole new kind of prehistoric creature!

Ichthyosaurus was about the size of a grown human.

Mary loved fossil hunting so much that she became a paleontologist. She found many more important fossils, such as Plesiosaurus, another ocean reptile. She also found Pterodactylus macronyx, a flying reptile.

At first many paleontologists did not give Mary credit for her fossil finds. They did not want to believe that a young girl could be such a great fossil hunter. But by the time she died in 1847, Mary Anning was known as one of the greatest paleontologists in the world.

Plesiosaurus

Pterodactylus

Digging for Fossils

Finding fossils is fun and exciting. But it is also hard work. Paleontologists really "rough it." The weather can be boiling hot or freezing cold. Strong winds can blow a whole camp away.

Every day on a dig seems long. Fossil hunters crawl on the ground, searching for good places to dig. Then they get to work with shovels, picks, brushes, and other tools.

Sometimes paleontologists spend many days sifting through dirt. Sometimes they spend a whole day searching and find nothing. Other times they discover large bones. Scientists harden the bones with a special glue.

Then the bones are carefully wrapped in heavy cloth and plaster of Paris. When the cast dries, the fossils are ready to be taken back to a museum.

Paleontologists carefully break the cast and cut it open. Then they gently blow or brush away the sand and dirt from the bones. They clean the bones. Then they glue any broken pieces into place. Whole dinosaur skeletons are rare. Sometimes paleontologists find bits and pieces of different skeletons. When they have enough parts, they are ready to put a whole dinosaur skeleton together!

Young people digging for fossils

Types of Ichthyosaurs

Many kinds of ichthyosaurs swam the seas hundreds of millions of years ago. A few of the known ichthyosaurs are shown on pages 28 and 29.

An ichthyosaur skeleton

Name	Size (length)	Period
Mixosaurus	3 feet (1 meter)	Triassic
Cymbospondylus	33 feet (10 meters)	Triassic
Shonisaurus	49 feet (15 meters)	Triassic
Stenopterygius	9 feet (2.7 meters)	Jurassic

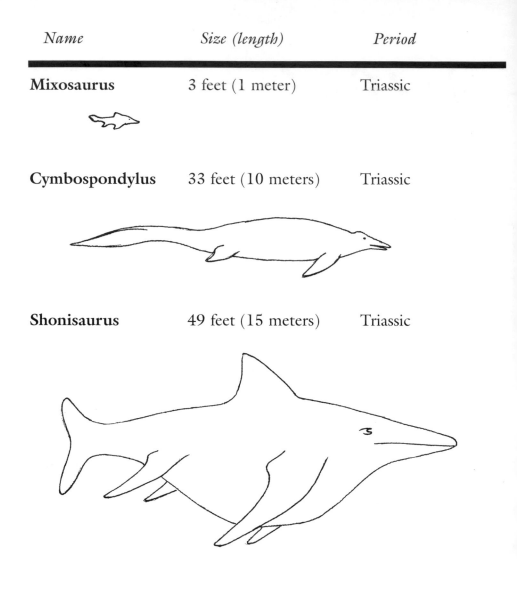

Name	Size (length)	Period
Ophthalmosaurus	11.5 feet (3.5 meters)	Jurassic
Eurhinosaurus	7 feet (2 meters)	Jurassic
Temnodontosaurus	30 feet (9 meters)	Jurassic
Ichthyosaurus	6 feet (1.8 meters)	Jurassic/Cretaceous

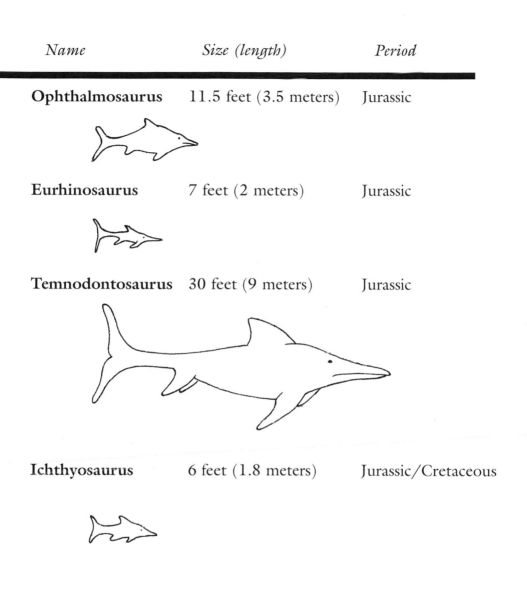

Scale 1 inch = 10 feet

Glossary

Cretaceous period (kreh-TAY-shus) The time period from 145 million to 65 million years ago

dinosaurs (DIE-nuh-sores) Land-dwelling reptiles that lived from 245 million to 65 million years ago

dorsal fin (DOR-sull fin) A fin on the back of a fish or water animal

fossil (FAH-sill) Remains of ancient life, such as a dinosaur bone, a footprint, or imprint in a rock

ichthyosaur (IK-thee-uh-sore) The group of ocean-dwelling reptiles to which Ichthyosaurus belonged

Ichthyosaurus (ik-thee-uh-SORE-us) An ocean-dwelling reptile that lived during the Jurassic and Cretaceous periods

Jurassic period (ju-RAS-ik) The time period from 208 million to 145 million years ago

meteorite (MEE-tee-uh-rite) A rocky object from space that strikes the earth's surface; it can be a few inches or several miles wide

paleontologist (pay-lee-on-TAH-luh-jist) A scientist who studies fossils

prehistoric (PREE-his-tor-ik) The time before written history

reptile (REP-tile) A group of air-breathing animals that lay eggs and usually have scaly skin

Triassic period (try-AS-ik) The time period from 245 million to 208 million years ago

Index

0/4 3/02 9-3-04